W9-CHS-234

rues

Poems
By
Philip Kobylarz

BLUE LIGHT PRESS ✦ 1ST WORLD PUBLISHING

1st WORLD
PUBLISHING

SAN FRANCISCO ✦ FAIRFIELD ✦ DELHI

Winner of the 2011 Blue Light Book Award

rues

Copyright ©2011 by Philip Kobylarz

All rights reserved. Printed in the United States of America. No part of this book may be used or reproduced in any manner whatsoever without written permission except in the case of brief quotations embodied in critical articles and reviews. For information contact:

1st WORLD LIBRARY
809 S. 2nd Street
Fairfield, Iowa 52556
www.1stworldpublishing.com

BLUE LIGHT PRESS
1563 45th Avenue
San Francisco, California, 94122

BOOK & COVER DESIGN
Melanie Gendron
www.melaniegendron.com

COVER AND AUTHOR PHOTO
Philip Kobylarz

FIRST EDITION

LCCN: 2011961446

ISBN 9781421886367

for, always,
Gitane
& now &
forever,
Karina

acknowledgments

chiffre *Colorado Review*

counterfeit, novella *The Louisville Review*

no angels *Common Ground*

Luberon, the secret of architecture,
card celebrating Arbor Day *Notre Dame Review*

contents

avenue du point d'interrogation

prelude

no angels

The place in which we live, that landscape seen
in the window frame, moveable and tipped
as it sometimes is in fallen clouds of snow,
is never really out there. All views are interiors.

boulevard du lapin blanc

traffic

Where there were birds, now buildings.
And the heels of uneaten bread. Out
the window, billboards and other signs
of attempted comprehension. Drapes
patterned with a table and flower pot.
Ancient or modern, streets go one way:
back.

coffers

Rug pattern woven with hair. Footprints
of insects in the flour. Value of old stamps
or money hidden in the linen. If feelings
could be saved in a box, we, most assuredly,
would hide it under the stairs.

trails

Sea's only rival: clouds on a perfect day.
Mountain's only friends are rocks; trees
grow in them. We walk a path marked
by red swaths of blood, or paint, to find
nothing and the teepee of bones it left behind.

chiffre

With trains, books, enemies, the mail,
dirty dishes, and the next meal, grass,
soap, dead birds, check stubs, promises
on windy days, clouds and handkerchiefs,
paperwork and bottles of wine, there's always more.

the secret of architecture

Time in between rains, a melon wrapped
in foil. We walk from one antique dealer
to another with a box of dusty crucifixes
to sell. Why buildings without inhabitants
crumble. Nothing to hold them down.

white rabbit boulevard

The lonely dog barks at sounds, all night.
Throw it a piece of bread, for silence.
In the chapel, there's a fresco portraying
miraculous snow. The priest's breath smells
of parchment. He shakes our hands, twice.

novella

Wind visits by slamming a window.
In so many days, not much to occur.
We varnish the table, a hope for rain.
The bakery is closed which is something
everyone knows. Monday morning, urgently
leashed dogs leave hoodoos of shit on the street.

queue

Day begins in eternity, burnt bread
and an audience of sparrows. Returning
in September. A will is modified to include
the newborn. So many keys to unlocked doors.
Laundry hangs, in attendance, waiting to be worn.

meantime

Sun pools on the tiles. Potted plants
stretch their roots. Beware of dog sign
is now in use. Promenade of traffic
has stalled, going somewhere. The bar
opens. Only customers — bees.

after thought

An annex containing histories of shoes
and purses no longer walked. Brilliant
autumn light on skin. Regrets of flowers,
having bloomed. Bread baked to be torn
apart. At the bistro, waiters wait under
sycamores, women talk of their new, blonde hair.

randonnée

So many snail shells in the sand
suggest a desert, the graveyard it hides.
Rocks grow into trees, the light echoes;
a valency, whatever it might be, happens.
At the pass, painted graffiti, expected to be
primal and in another language.

penitence

Seagulls, really mutes, try to talk
while what we hear is begging. The park
is cluttered with people and the flags
of plastic they leave. If the word for sin
is peach tree, there is no redemption.

diurnal

Posters re-postered. New music comes, is played,
goes. Children, locked in school, wait
to erupt in energy that running cures. The bus
empties itself at urinals of stops. Dogs parade
home, attending corners, select trees and corners,
knowing exactly where they are going.

then the bombs

Old things are painted white, the simplest
color of resurrection. The view from the *pissoire*
is nearly the same picture everyday, a study
of realism. Boredom hits the big city in waves,
nothing to do but kill.

card celebrating Arbor Day

Whatever the weather, pages in time layers,
there's what's seen from *l'Estaque*. Any book
or geographic dictionary in the crudeness
of a public library: cold magazines, maps of
an east, books used. Grocery lists better left
unread. Great places to go– where you already
are, just without the same, swaying, trees.

quiet clocks

Old photos in another language,
the people look vaguely the same
Separated at birth, families cling
to umbilical cords of memory, powdered
thought collects in luggage stored
in rooms. Nothing is kept safe.

tambourines

The rest being simplification, a pruning
of the *citronnier* branches, crusts
from bread left for pigeons, thread
and needle unattached. Men in the street
smile to each other; coins, sad faces of,
making music in their pockets.

logic

A painted stairway, first step
to the last, going up. Resulting in
footprints or not anywhere to go.
Rains came leaving calling cards
of leaves. Snails try to enter
an empty fishbowl.

greenhouse

Clover grows in the abandoned
pot. The baker creases his dough
with a screwdriver. Bests secrets
aren't ones kept. They're the ones
everyone knows.

le temps

What pigeons do at night, still
a mystery. On the roof, there's
a pile of thread and key chains. View
of the ocean is the same: blue plains.
A puddle of sky with waves.

Luberon

Bird of unknown origin. Castles
were built so we could walk their
ruins. In the mysterious hills, grapes
are free. Surprised by an accumulation
of stones, we find a cemetery for two,
the plot of every happy story.

argent

Though coins are few, they weigh
more than they can buy. Though coins
are few, they ring pleasant in the hand.
Few are the coins, for buying time.
Though coins are few, they are worth
their fleeting weight, not in paper, only gold.

allée des chèvrefeuilles

meridians

October at the beach and they are still
swimming. To parachute, one must first
practice. Ladies expose their backs to us,
their breasts to the sun. A haze envelopes
the city we don't want to see anyway.

arrival

She keeps with her countless souvenirs
of Lourdes, medallions, candles, coffee cups,
playing cards, stacks of old, empty shoe boxes.
Not knowing she will die one day and that
these are, waiting in the wings, coffins.

departure

When the garbage trucks come, no praise
is offered, no one waves goodbye, nothing
is missed, the men are anonymous in their
soiled jumpsuits. We part with the things
we once loved. The noise is expected.

brine

News is a flower that has bloomed.
In the port, boats embark to distant
islands, other ports. Bells ring and
bells ring unanswered. The metro smells
like a sea underground. Police
wait for bombs to never explode.

counterfeit

Fake coins for months are passed
and used. Until the word gets out
and no where will accept. A bum says
if they're not real, then sell me
                    imaginary cigarettes.

attendance

Wine for sale cheaper than bottled water.
Dogs driven wild by scents wait outside
the grocery store. Petted by an array
of hands, they relinquish themselves
to the leash of old leather, familiarity.

bounty

Hills are rending clouds again, there's
nothing better for the weather to do.
Arbousier blooms spiked red candies
of fruit, free for the taking. In the city,
the cemetery is empty with visitors.

another century

Opened, behind steel curtains,
storefronts. Windows, baked goods,
magazines, people. Saracen of the night
in hiding. Each building, a castle remembered.

arboretum

Arguments on the streets occur inevitably
beneath windows drawn with sleep.
Less sirens than horns. Trees in the park
already have begun their silent march.

premonition

Lonely man who lives downstairs
waits on the corner wearing ironed
slacks. It's Friday night. His hair
is parted in hopes it won't remain so.

silver screen

Sea has made just claim to the view
and filled the city with its margin.
Notes are scribbled and abandoned.
She was once a model, we remember
as she sees us, trying to conceal groceries,
pulled by a cart, with her still thin body.

hex

The ladder must be returned to Elise
who will say a few words to gain some
in return. We both pretend to understand.
The room fills with the purple smell
and sight of a tart borne from the oven.

canada gris

Vegetable stand swarms with those
expecting guests. Vendors brag about
flavors of produce from Spain. A child
eats grapes straight from the crate,
everyone tries their hardest not to notice.

bel canto

Songs, old songs, from an old country,
say Sardinia, played and sung over
the airwaves. Grandparents around
a t.v. set. A most harmless kind
of death, nostalgia is.

race

If he looks like what he is,
a certain time-honored nationality,
Corsican or Dutch, he's said to have
that type of head. Streets fill
with the anonymity of *pieds-noirs*.

pilgrimage

A raid of pigeons tapping at the windows.
Stones are thrown to scare them away.
Pillar of bread, pillar of cement, pillar
of pepper, pillar of pillars rotting to sand.

novelty

Fountain in the park endlessly,
until winter, flowing. Children ride
new bikes, looking for new friends,
new toys, trails, new birds and brush animals,
stopping to talk to different parents.

small worlds

In the depth of night, movement
is heard in the kitchen, a tinkering.
Washed dishes, silverware, a *quignon*
of bread, bugs inventorying old discoveries.

fallow

Cherries, unpicked, fall to the ground
and split open with ripeness. Dogs
come down with colic. Under the tree,
a pig farm of living ruins.

Notre Dame

The bus waits for us. At the post office,
the worker is sympathetic, offers a choice
of overseas stamps. No line at the bakery.
On her perch, the golden lady casts
her lot of daily, mute miracles.

fable

Throughout the night, a machine hums,
creates a stream of foam in the street.
Dogs don't sleep, cats are agitated.
Across the *pêcherie*, bones of mermaids wash by.

robber baron

On the roof: inevitable black cat
wearing a white tie. Motionless,
it waits for birds and butterflies
hungry not for food, but a murder.

clues

Mingled on the street with everything
else, a water soaked baguette, clothespins,
empty box of cigarettes, fallen fruit,
a braid of hair cut at the barber's.

chemin de la femme morte

Saints' Day

These hills that are by-lines
meandering through the past,
stop in the present. Haze apparent,
the day, without gloom, a see-through.

scourge

Wind again, searches the alley in complete
disregard to the hazard it makes. Cats
disappear. Windows break. Birds disdain
the sky. Babies can't breathe. All hats
off to November's calling card, blown away.

speculation

A finite row of plowed sugar, the sea
in wind. It is speculated that there
are cave paintings in it, under it. It
is speculated there is snow in heaven.

risk

Small house abandoned, the corner of the street
walled with stone, broken glass, futile
barbed wire stretched into shapes of prospectors
looking for treasure, a dress-maker's dummy.

quick sand

Linseed oil painted on tile and left
to capture footprints, leaves, flowers
bloomed and spilt, feathers of magpies,
ashes, the jewel of a false tooth.

functionaries

A certain hour, daily, co-mingling
scents of dinner. Music and clattering
of dishes, tonight a feast. Signs
remind us that government offices
are closed for days. Early Monday morning,
they'll get back to planning holidays.

gargoyles

Coldness descends and sticks to streets
like litter, mostly un-wrappings. Men smoke
more, women walk faster wearing black
leather, returning to their second skins.

lost and

The story goes: she went to Toulouse
to meet some friends. Story goes:
she never came back. With so many
pictures of her, on buildings, the news,
the time is filled looking, missing.

in memory

Shots of hunters resound in the empty
wildness. Hills, these cliffs that breach
into villages, sometimes cities crowned
with castle or church and enveloped
in lavender and lumps of unseen poison.

pomp

Because space must be conserved,
families are buried on top of each
other, each person a level of history.
On the tomb are plaques that read:
in memory, without you, souvenir.

stasis

It's a querulous affair: when to return
the ladder. In between appointments
with the doctor, daily visits to the fruit
stand, expected unexpected callings
from neighbors, the day is passed
as if there were really something to be done.

vesper

In youth, she posed as a nun. How many,
many photos wearing a wooden cross, hands
clasped in sincerity, lips pressed together, ironed
white habit, hair concealed as cloth.

repast

Her husband fell while climbing
a mountain; she keeps pictures
of him on the walls, has sold
or given away his possessions.
She takes meals on the terrace,
with a view of the low Alps,
where he is now somewhere
beyond, across her, an empty plate.

spoils

A minimum of labor is done, but
accomplished her way. She waits for
just the right time to hand over a bag
of cookies, small cakes, a bottle of
lotion, and a rabbit's head for the dog.

modeling

She is old now but her hands
are still young, being a seamstress
in her spare time. She asks a customer
to try on the skirt, we are both busy
with work, separated by a sudden nudity.

circumstance

He picks apples in Italy, when in season,
working every other day, the year
was bad. From Hungary, he waits
in doorways, collecting money
he'll share, half and half, with the whores.

catacomb

No bones about it: lunch hour,
streets are alive with hunger.
In front of the sandwich shop
a line of impatient speculators;
wooden crates bloodied with hooves.

direction millaud

Her façade, the oldest in the village,
something for which she is proud.
On Sunday evenings, at the piano
practicing music and being alone.

fête

Holidays of another country pass
by, here we celebrate the return
of winter birds. *Mésange* on the
doorstep, seeking the origin of crumbs.

le terminus

End of the district: a church and bus
stop. There's the regulars, men in hats,
kids going to school, pigeons waiting
for a ride, and Christ hanging around.

left unsaid

One large, not too bad, nude
hangs on the wall, covered in haste
by an old textile, creases can be seen
in both. We are guests of another sort.

avenue du point d'interrogation

noon hour

Rather do nothing. Than have nothing
to do. Finally, no rain lasting for days.
Kids from Catholic school light up
outside the walls, hurrying to be adults.
Scooters zooming towards afternoons
of television, parents at work, and sex.

fenders

There's not much to say, so they yell.
Body language is *commedia dell'arte*.
The cars suffer minor scratches in
an accident. The people, for the given
moment, act as who they are: lovers.

mannerism

In the bar there's always more smoke
than inspiration. So the waitress
bends at the waist to replace
a napkin on the table, noticing
her body every inch as much as you do.

difference

Incremental. Four fish for dinner.
At the hospital where Rimbaud died,
the plaque goes mostly unread. And in
photography books of nudes, the pictures
are there, never torn out, defiled, stolen.

champignons

That her breasts are blooming
with a fungus of nervousness
referred to as mushrooms, she walks
the rain dampened hills and a trail
studded with so many reminders.

vaisselle

Claiming the black under her finger–
nails is blood from the hearts
of artichokes, she continues with
dinner, then the dishes, with dirty hands.

marseilleveyre

Summit is stumbled upon
as a crown, a cross, a fallen
cross. Hills are white with
envy: they will never die.

le monde

What is not usual is merely coincidence.
Those who don't gamble appear when
there are stakes, with umbrellas. Glory
is as thick as coats of paint on white
windows. Gathering around kiosks to hear
the papers speak of a stolen plane that
flew through the legs of the Eiffel tower again.

solstice

That mimosas are in bloom,
it may be spring. Turquoise, blue
waves, or anemones. Winter
has left the beach, leaving
behind its bra, and one leather shoe.

blasphemy

Hours of the park when no
one visits. These noons of strays:
cats, dogs, people. Koi
of no particular gender.

obisbo

Pillows on a make shift bed,
vegetable crates and wool
stuffed mattress. Hastily sewn
together, in canvass, they molt.
With each sleeping, feathers.

canebière

Seeming to never rain again,
fish merchants proudly display
their stock. Blue crabs and white
mussels, ropes salted by the sea.
Reality almost ready to eat.

secret garden

on the sides of roads they
present themselves as weeds,
these flowers of early March:
never so many dandelions, forget-
me-nots, strange red ones sung *coquelicots*.

en route

In any given instance, an argument.
About mail, unpaid water bills,
the left open-ness of a door.
So much civilization built into walls,
and rain soaking history in mud.

perturbation

Whether or not the bus will come
is not known. Time shared
tapping watches, wondering about
shapes of feet fitted in shoes.

amants

Lovers here offer no exception,
they hairpin the beach and lawn
bordering. In the park they lie in
open theaters of their, and our, desire.

vernal

Wild irises in yellow and purple,
acacia around the aqueduct
as if it were Hiram's grave.
Laughter in the chalk hills, of gulls;
flesh the color of sand. Spring.

folly

From afar, women in tight black
pants at the beach, really only girls.
Boys run in packs, shouting loud
as the colors of their shorts, already
men. The promise of sex, better broken.

beau soleil

Enjoying cigarettes in the sun,
seasoned women in the almost nude.
Threes of slow burning aureoles.

unsaid

In a pot on the roof long forgotten
bloom weeds and their flowers:
soucis, pensées. Better to leave
worries & thoughts, alone.

kept

Because it stormed so much
we collected it in buckets
and were reminded by
a plastic bottled labeled rain.

grotesquerie

Anxious people leave doors
to get what's necessary:
lilies on the first of May,
sticks of bread protected by
bats on handles, broken umbrellas.

immortality

In a jar, no – a glass made
for drinking she has kept
cuttings of her finger & toe
nails for these past thirty
years. To prove, perhaps, or
measure, how she has grown.

May Day

The first of May when
everyone, it seems, is seen
with freshly bought lilies-
of-the-valley. When the hill-
sides bloom in downpours of flowers.

retour, le temps

Warm day in winter distinguishable
by traffic and the number of pedestrians
and a flock of sparrows dotting the sky
perceptible. In a rain of bird shit.

vagary

From here on out the things
that remain are the same:
chain pull toilet, a smell,
remarkable, of burning soap.

glossary

boulevard du lapin blanc white rabbit boulevard

chiffre number or a taking account

randonnée hiking

pissoire an outdoor bathroom, often basically a metal wall with a small
section cut out as a "window"

citronnier lemon tree

le temps the weather

Lubéron a region in the south of France known for its grapes and
presided over by Mt. Ventoux

argent money

allée des chèvrefeuilles honeysuckle alley

arbousier often translated as "strawberry tree" but the fruits are more
lychee-like

canada gris grey Canada: a type of apple

bel canto Italian for beautiful singing

pieds-noirs literally "black feet"– French citizens whose parents were
born in Algeria

quignon Provencal derived word for the very tip or ends of a baguette

pêcherie small store where fish/seafood is sold fresh

chemin de la femme morte passage way of the dead woman

repast meal

direction millaud towards the street Millaud

fête celebration

mésange titmous

avenue du point d'interrogation question mark avenue

commedia dell'arte Italian for the comedy of the art of improvisation

vaisselle the dishing as in washing the dishes

marseilleveyre famous mountain that overlooks southern Marseille

le monde the world

obisbo bishop

canebière main street of downtown Marseille it's named derived from
cannabis referring to main source of rope in the past

coquelicots poppies

en route on one's way to a destination

amants lovers

beau soleil beautiful sunshine or great weather

soucis, pensées worries, thoughts

retour, le temps the weather returning

About the Author

P hilip Kobylarz's poems, essays, and short stories appear in such journals as *The Iowa Review, Paris Review,* and *Massachusetts Review.* Currently he is engaged in the study of how to be/not be.

Printed in the United States of America

CPSIA information can be obtained at www.ICGtesting.com
Printed in the USA
LVOW111107280212

270732LV00001B/8/P